THE
6TH SENSE . . .
FAITH

by John Osteen

Lakewood Church
P.O. Box 23297
Houston, TX 77228

ISBN 0-912631-12-0

THE 6TH SENSE...
FAITH

Several years ago a friend of mine was flying at 35,000 feet in a jet on his way to a preaching appointment. Let me share a little bit about this friend of mine, who is now traveling throughout the world fulfilling the ministry God has given him. This man was an accomplished pianist. He was such a tremendous artist in this area of music that he was offered opportunities in the entertainment world that would have assured him a great future in that area of life alone. He also had a beautiful solo voice. His musical talents were superb. God had called him to preach and he had chosen to follow the vocation which was the perfect will of God for his life. Through the years he had endeavored to be faithful to God.

At this time as he flew in an airplane on his way to preach the Gospel, he found himself in a very peculiar and unusual situation. Several years before this airplane trip he was afflicted with what the medical world termed as Rheumatoid Arthritis. This grew progressively worse in his entire body. His hands became knotted and gnarled and paralyzed to free movement. So, his days of artistry at the piano were gone forever. All the joints of his body were affected by this disease. His ankles were swollen to the size of grapefruit. His knees were enlarged. All of his joints were filled with pain.

He was unable to function in a normal way. He told me that he didn't buy aspirin by the box, he bought it by the case. He took it constantly to try to relieve the excruciating pain that was throughout his body.

He also said that many mornings he had to be rolled out of bed with the help of others and placed in a tub of hot water. He would stay there for a while in order to be able to function at all during the day time. This would seemingly loosen up the joints and partially relieve the pain. His body became stooped. He was not able to walk in a normal fashion but simply made his way along the best he could with his knees and ankles and the rest of his joints aching and deformed by this unusual disease.

This was his condition as he sat on the airplane going to preach the Gospel.

The doctors had given him the verdict that there was no hope. There was nothing that medical science could do for him as far as there being any permanent healing. He could only get relief from the pain by taking medication. They told him that he would just simply have to live with it and gradually grow worse.

Gone was his ability to thrill and bless people with piano music. Gone was his ability to walk and to live a normal life. But he sat on that airplane, determined to go preach the Gospel to the best of his ability in this condition.

He related to me what happened to him on that airplane. Actually, a miracle took place. Oh, the world could not see the miracle. Those around him were not aware of the miracle. But nevertheless, a miracle took place. While reading his Bible on the airplane, he began to meditate on the scriptures. He saw that Jesus bore our sicknesses and carried our pains and by His stripes we are healed. (Isaiah 53:5) He read in Matthew 8:17 that Jesus healed all the sick, "That it might be fulfilled which was spoken by

Esaias the prophet, saying, Himself took our infirmities, and bare our sicknesses." He read in I Peter 2:24, "Who His own self bare our sins in His own body on the tree, that we, being dead to sins, should live unto righteousness: by whose stripes ye were healed."

Suddenly, a light turned on deep on the inside of him. He heard in his inner man the words, "By His stripes *YOU WERE HEALED.*" There came a true understanding on the inside of him as he rode 35,000 feet in the air. Suddenly, he knew that he was healed! Suddenly, he had absolute assurance that he was free from that disease. He began to rejoice because he knew he was healed.

As he sat there on the airplane with this revelation knowledge that he was healed, he didn't look any different, his body didn't feel any different, his body didn't function any differently, but he knew that he was healed. He knew that a miracle had taken place on the inside.

When he got off of the airplane, he could barely make it out of the seat. He hobbled down the aisle. Someone met him at the airplane. Actually, it was the pastor from the church who met him at the gate at the airport. He took his little case from him and said, "Brother, how are you?" And my friend seemingly filled with rheumatoid arthritis, still stooped over, still hobbling along with aching joints, still even unable to look up in a normal fashion; but as he bent over and hobbled along, he turned his head slightly (as much as he could) to look upward toward the pastor, and said, "Oh, I'm glad to announce to you that I'm healed by the stripes of Jesus."

Of course, the pastor wondered if not only his body had been affected by the disease, but maybe his mind also!

The time came for my friend to minister at the pastor's church. He hobbled to the platform and stood behind the pulpit. In this same condition, with the arthritis seemingly still dominating his body, he looked up at the congregation and said, "Before I open the Bible and preach the message to you, I would like to make a confession. I would like to rejoice before all of you. I would like to tell you that I am so glad that the Lord Jesus Christ has healed my body. I am so glad that by the stripes of Jesus I have been healed. I want you to rejoice with me that I am healed. Arthritis can not live in my body. My joints are well. Rejoice with me that I am a normal person, that I can play the piano again. I can walk normally again. I want you to rejoice with me that I am healed."

Each person in that congregation reacted in a different way. I am sure many of them wondered about the credibility of the man standing in the pulpit.

But, to tell you the end of the story, the man began to get better and better and better and better. And in a matter of a few weeks, all arthritis was gone from his body. Every joint was normal. He could play the piano. He was perfectly normal. That was well over twenty years ago. I have been in his meetings personally and wept as he played the piano and sang the songs of Zion and gave praise to the Lord Jesus Christ. Truly he is living a normal life even to this day!

Now what happened on the airplane?

Is there a law that can supercede the laws that we know of in the natural realm?

Is there something that we don't know as far as our natural minds are concerned? What really happened there on the airplane?

The Bible talks about the law of faith. The Bible talks about the law of the Spirit of life making us free from the law of sin and death. You see, sitting on that airplane, this friend received knowledge in his spirit-man that the world is unable to receive with the natural, carnal mind.

The Bible says that faith is of the heart. Romans 10:10 says, "With the heart man believeth ..." It is with your heart that you believe. The heart means the spirit-man. There is a spirit-man on the inside of your physical body. The Lord Jesus is telling us by inspiration of the Holy Spirit through the Apostle Paul, that faith is a spiritual force. Faith is a force that comes forth from the spirit-man. It is the spirit-man who is able to respond to the Word of God and to exercise faith.

Faith is of the heart.

Faith is a spirit force.

"With the heart man believeth ..."

You see, as that man sat on the airplane, filled with a disease that had crippled him and which would have held him captive throughout his life, he meditated on the Word of God. He read the promises of God. He read the great statements of God concerning the eternal redemption that we have in the Lord Jesus Christ. He read it and meditated on it until suddenly it was not only in his mind. It was not only his carnal mind meditating upon it, but his spirit-man began to pick up these truths. His inner man began to feed upon the things of God, who Himself is a Spirit.

It was Spirit to spirit communication.

When his spirit began to pick up the eternal facts of God's redemption from physical disease, things began to happen.

Suddenly when his spirit heard, "by His stripes ye were healed", faith leaped into being because faith is of the heart. It is with the heart man believeth. This man suddenly knew, not with his mind, but with his heart, with his spirit-man. He knew that he was healed. In this knowing, he was unshakable in his confidence. He had heard from God who is a Spirit, in his spirit, who is the real man.

Now his body looked just the same. His body responded just the same. His body gave no evidence that there was any change in him. Yet deep within himself he knew that he was healed.

You see, there is a sixth sense. The body has five senses. There is sight. There is hearing. There is taste, smell and touch. Five senses. And with these natural senses, we contact the physical world.

But there is another sense.

Surely if God has given the physical body five senses to contact and function in the natural, material world, then He has given the spirit-man, made alive with the life of Almighty God, some sort of a sense to function in the spirit realm. Yes! The spirit-man made alive by the grace and resurrection life of Jesus Christ, does have a sense. We call that sense faith.

Faith is totally independent of the five senses we use to function in the physical and material world.

This is what happened to the man on the airplane: He left the natural and went into the supernatural. He left the physical and went into the spiritual. He got out of his physical nature and got into his spiritual nature. That one sense of faith feeding on the Word of God, received revelation knowledge and received an unshakable confidence that he was truly healed. Though all of his physical senses denied it, and there was no evidence anywhere in his physical senses to corroborate the fact that he was healed, this one sense of faith which he would not give up, dominated and conquered all others! And his body responded. Sickness and disease left him. Today after more than twenty years, he is still functioning normally because of the law of faith.

Do you need a miracle today?

Do you realize that there is hope? It is possible for you to rise out of your prison house!

Jesus said, "With men this is impossible; but with God all things are possible." (Matthew 19:26) Jesus said this to encourage our hearts. As you look at your situation today, is it impossible with men? Is it impossible for you to be healed? Is it impossible for your family to be put back together? Is it impossible for that situation to be resolved? Do all the voices of relatives and doctors and professional men and friends say the word "impossible" to you? Then hear the sweet voice of the Son of God who cannot lie: "The things that are impossible with men are possible with God."

This is what this book is all about. It will tell you how you can function in a sixth sense called faith. You can shake off the shackles that hold you in the realm of the natural and touch God who is in the realm of the supernatural.

This book will teach you how to be conscious of two worlds, the visible world and the invisible world. You will learn how you can contact and function in the law of the invisible, where there are no impossibilities.

My friends, my heart rejoices in knowing that you are going to find the help and the miracle that you need.

Our own family is filled with miracles today as a result of the truth that I am going to share with you in this book. My wife, who is a registered nurse, could vividly describe our daughter, Lisa, who was born over twenty years ago abnormally. The pediatrician said she had cerebral palsy. She had no sucking reflexes. She had no muscle tone. She had no ability to crawl. She had no strength in her body. And the word "impossible"was written over her life. Our hearts were saddened. There seemed no way that she would ever have an opportunity to live a normal life. We faced this situation and put the laws and principles of God presented in this book into effect.

As we began to function in God, we found even as that minister on the airplane did, the eternal truths of God. They illuminated understanding on the inside of us. We began to rejoice that she was healed. We prayed the prayer of faith. We anointed her with oil. Though there was no change in her body, though it looked as though she would forever be abnormal, yet in our spirit-man, our spirit nature declared that we had the confidence that Lisa had been healed by the stripes of the Lord Jesus Christ.

Everything about her screamed out, "No, no, no, she's not normal."

Yet, we had a knowing on the inside of us.

Every one of our five senses cried out, "No, no, no, she is not healed."

Yet that one dominant sense in our spirit nature called faith, that has revelation knowledge from God, overcame all of the natural senses!

I am glad to announce to you that after twenty-two years (at this writing) our daughter remains normal and healed. She became normal as a little child. She lived a normal life through grade school, middle school, high school, and through college. I thank God she is normal and well this day — simply because there is a sixth sense called faith.

Faith feeds upon the Word of God. Faith is of the heart.

I could relate to you many, many miracles in the lives of our other children, in my life, and in my wife's life, that have come as a result of functioning in this sixth sense.

Let me encourage you to meditate on the Word of God.

Study the truths presented in this book until you too can rise up above the word "impossible". Begin to function in the realm of faith.

Faith is of the heart.

Meditate upon these truths until they get beyond your carnal mind.

Meditate upon these truths until they get down into your spirit.

In your spirit-man receive them as revelation knowledge from God who is a Spirit.

Strive in your meditation to have the communication of Spirit to spirit. (That is, your spirit communicating and listening and responding to God who is a Spirit.)

Let's look at the Word of God as we proceed with these truths in this book. Begin to rejoice even now that God will give you the desires of your heart.

In Genesis 1:1-3: "In the beginning God prepared, formed, fashioned, and created the heavens and the earth. The earth was without form and an empty waste, and darkness was upon the face of the very great deep. The Spirit of God was moving, hovering, brooding over the face of the waters. And God said, Let there be light; and there was light."

We read in Hebrews chapter 11, verse 3, "By faith we understand that the worlds were framed, fashioned, put in order and equipped for their intended purpose by the Word of God, so that what we see was not made out of things which are visible."

These scriptures teach us about joining hands with the Creator. God our Father is a creator. Jeremiah said, "Ah, Lord God! behold, thou hast made the heaven and the earth by Thy great power and stretched out arm, and there is nothing is too hard for Thee." (Jer. 32:17)

We know that Jesus is a creator. Colossians 1:16 says, "For it was in Him that all things were created, in heaven and on earth, things seen and things unseen, whether thrones, dominions, rulers or authorities; all things were created and exist through Him (by His service, intervention) and in and for Him.''

John 1:1-3 says that Jesus was the co-creator of the universe.

We know that the Holy Spirit is a creator.

We are in God's class and we belong to God's family. God expects us to have creative ability. We are to join hands with the Creator. We are co-laborers with God in creating things in our day.

In Hebrews 11:3 it says, "We understand that the worlds were framed, fashioned, put in order and equipped for their intended use by the Word of God, so that what we see was not made out of things that are visible ." (Amplified Bible)

You have your own little world. Everybody has his own world. While some of us may be rejoicing today, your little world may be shattered. It may be like the world was in the beginning; it was without form and void and darkness was upon the face of the deep. (Gen. 1:2) It may well be that this is the way you are today, that your world is without form. It is filled with chaos and darkness.

Thank God your world can be reframed!

Your world can be refashioned!

Your world can be equipped for its intended purpose!

This is done by the Word of God and out of the invisible forces of God.

Look again at Hebrews 11:3: "We understand that what is seen ..." What is seen? The stars, the moon, the sun, the earth, the trees, the dirt, the flowers, the grass, the clouds. The Bible says that what we see was *not* made out of things which are visible. What we see was made out of invisible things. What we see in this natural world was really made out of invisible forces. Hebrews 11:3 is talking about two worlds—there is a seen world and an unseen world. There must be a visible world and an invisible world. There must be a material world and a spiritual world. The Bible says that what you see in the physical, material realm was not made out of things that you could see, but made out of the invisible. It is unique that God would begin this faith chapter like that. The Creator of the universe started with invisible forces. He started in the unseen area. He started in the spiritual dimension. All of the creative building blocks of God are in another dimension—the invisible world.

THE CREATIVE BUILDING BLOCKS THAT WE NEED FOR CREATION ARE NOT IN THIS MATERIAL DIMENSION.

They are in another dimension. God has building blocks. He has creative material that all of us can use, but the creative material of God is not in the material universe. His building blocks are out there in the invisible, unseen, spiritual world.

THE THINGS THAT ARE SEEN
ARE NOT MADE OUT OF THINGS VISIBLE,
BUT OF THINGS INVISIBLE.

Faith is our sixth sense to contact the greater dimension of reality. Hebrews 11:1, ''Now faith is the assurance, the confirmation, the title-deed of things we hope for, being the proof of things we do not see (this is talking about invisible forces) and the conviction of their reality — faith perceiving as real fact what is not revealed to the senses."

Faith created by the Word of God perceives as real fact that which is not revealed to our natural senses!

There are five senses in the human body. They are seeing, tasting, smelling, hearing and touching. We touch, we smell, we see, we hear, we taste. These are all in the natural world. We use these senses to contact this natural world. God gave you these five senses for use in the natural world.

But there is another sense, the sense of the spirit man on the inside of you, and that sense is called faith.

This sense of faith is used to touch the unseen, invisible world. The natural senses cannot touch that spiritual dimension. They have no contact with it. But faith, created by the Word of God, enables you to reach out into the dimension of the invisible and activate the creative power of God.

The Bible is like a great forest. Growing in that forest are the giant redwoods of God's eternal truths. We need to march out daily into this great forest and look at the giant, immovable redwood trees of God's eternal truths and bask in their presence. Then we can come back into the material world with revelation knowledge that Bible principles are eternally true.

Here is an illustration about your five senses. I will use my wife, Dodie, in this illustration. Dodie uses a special perfume. I can pass by Dodie, and one of my senses, the sense of smell, will alert me and tell me if she has on that perfume. I smell that perfume. One of my senses picks up the fact, "There is perfume here."

However, in the natural realm, my other four senses do not have any proof at all that the perfume is really there.

My eyes could say, "Perfume? I don't see it. You will never convince me anything is real that I can't see."

My ears could say, "I don't hear perfume. You will never convince me anything is real I can't hear."

"Perfume?" My hands could say, "I don't feel any perfume. You will never convince me anything is real if I can't feel it." My tongue could say, "I can't taste any perfume. There is no perfume here."

I could begin to think, "There is not any perfume here. I don't have it. I can't feel it. I can't hear it. I can't see it. I can't taste it."

But my nose could say, "You other senses be quiet! As the nose, I have already actually experienced the perfume. I have, with my sense of smell, confirmed its reality. It does not matter what you can't hear, and what you can't see, and what you can't taste, and what you can't touch. My ability to smell says, It is real, it is real! I have used my sense of smell to confirm that it is real. I announce to you, It is real!"

In this same way, I go out by my sense of faith into the Word of God—into the great forest of God—and meditate on what God says is mine in that invisible realm. I look at the great truths of Almighty God and with the sixth sense in my spirit-man, I believe and I have a consciousness that they are mine.

I see and believe salvation is mine.

Healing is mine.

Prosperity is mine. All of God's blessings are mine. On the basis of this information from the sixth sense of faith, I can confidently say, "I am healed! I am blessed! I am redeemed! I am prosperous!"

Now once you begin to act like the Word is true, your five natural senses will try to contradict the Word of God. Your five natural senses will say, "I can't touch it; I can't hear it; I can't see it; I can't feel it; I can't taste it; so I must not be healed. I must not be prosperous. I have looked into my pocketbook and my eyes see nothing. I have felt all over my body and the knots are still there.

My sense of touch and feeling tell me I am not healed. My eyes tell me I'm not prosperous. My ears tell me that I don't have it."

But you see, there is a spiritual principle at work. It is just like when I could smell Dodie's perfume. My sense of faith tells these five natural senses, "You five senses be quiet! I have been looking at God's eternal truths, and I have received revelation knowledge which is beyond you. I can assure you, though you have no other proof, it is a reality! God cannot lie!"

When your nose assures you of the evidence of perfume, all your other senses still have no way of proving there is perfume in the air.

Why should you allow your natural senses to have more integrity than Almighty God?

I want to tell you that the sense of smell in your nose does not have more integrity than God! Your nose could be wrong. It could be defective. But God cannot be defective.

Let us venture into the great forest of God's eternal truths and find out about His abundant blessings for us. We will discover that God has given us certain benefits. Our faith detects and confirms that they are ours. Our faith will meditate upon them.

Meditating on God's Word is the best way to get your faith to work. Faith comes by hearing, and hearing by the Word of God. (Romans 10:17) Live in the Word of God. Walk every day under the shade of the giant trees of God's eternal truths. Bask in the sunlight of God's spiritual world, and know that in that invisible dimension, *it is yours*. Your faith says it is yours.

Faith causes the written Word of God to become as an audible voice of God spoken to you personally. Meditate on it until suddenly you say, "I am saved. I am healed. I am rich. I am victorious. I am strong."

It makes no difference what the five senses in this natural realm say to you, your faith will perceive it as real fact.

The Bible says that God created material things out of things that are invisible. All our blessings come from the invisible world. Your redemption is spiritual. Forgiveness was invisible. How did I find out about that great invisible fact of forgiveness? I found out in the Word of God. It was invisible, but it became visible when I accepted it. Healing and prosperity dwell in the spiritual dimension, the invisible world. When we see it there in the Word of God, and our sixth sense of faith takes hold of it, then faith brings it over into the natural world.

Your senses will often try to contradict God's Word just like my four other senses were saying there was not any perfume present. But remember, my nose with its one little sense of smell convinced them all that it was there!

When we come back from God's great forest of eternal truths then faith shouts out, "I've got it! I've got it!" All the five senses might say, "You don't! You don't! You know you don't have it. Check any records of the doctor. Go have the medical tests taken. Go have an x-ray, it won't show it. The eyes won't see it. You don't feel it, you don't have it."

This is the battle ground. But remember, the battle is won when you listen to your spirit-man rejoicing over what he *knows* to be true through revelation knowledge gained from the Word of God by the sixth sense of FAITH!

In II Kings 6, this story is told. The Syrians were fighting the Israelites and every time the Syrians moved, the Israelites knew where they were. They would go down the road to plan an attack and the Israelites would be there. So the Syrian leader got all the people together and said, "I want to know something in this counsel of war. Who is for Israel and who is for us? There must be a spy in the camp."

They said, "No, there is not a spy in the camp but there is a prophet down in Israel. And what you whisper in your bedchamber he tells the king of Israel." (vs. 12)

This fellow said, "What you whisper in your bedchamber, they know." That is the way it is going to be with us. God is going to move by the supernatural. They said, "You mean there is a prophet down there that can understand these things?" Yes. Do you know what they did? They sent a whole army to get one man. That is how scared the devil is of Spirit-filled Christians. Elisha was at Dothan and they sent

17

an army down to Dothan in the night time, to get one man.

Can you imagine? You may not know it, but the devil is scared of you. The Bible says, "Resist the devil and he will flee (in terror) from you." The devil trembles at the very thought of you.

They sent an army down there after one man. Old Elisha was sleeping and he had a young man with him that reminds me of some today. The Bible says in verse 14, "Therefore sent he thither horses, and chariots, and a great host." Can you imagine a great host? And they came by night and encompassed the city. A host compassed the city both with horses and chariots and his servant said unto him, "Alas what shall we do?"

All this young man could see was this world and he became nervous and upset. He said, "Oh, what are we going to do?" I hear people today talking about famine and talking about pestilence and talking about all of the destruction coming on the world.

Well, it might come on some people, but it is not going to come on me! Praise God! I am blessed. God has not appointed me to wrath. He has appointed me to obtain salvation through the Lord Jesus Christ.

I can hear them talking about all this. They are wringing their hands, "What shall we do? What shall we do?"

Oh, this is a picture of the world today. "Alas, master what shall we do?"

Elisha gets up, walks out and says, "Let me survey the situation." He looks around and sees all those hundreds and possibly thousands of horses and chariots out there and said, "Oh, don't worry, they that be for us are more than they that be for them."

I can imagine that young man living today. He would have said, "Elisha, even by the new math, 1 and 1 makes 2, and we are out-numbered!"

Elisha said, "Lord, I pray thee, open his eyes that he may see. And the Lord opened the eyes of the young man; and he saw: and, behold, the mountain was full of horses and chariots of fire round about Elisha." (II Kings 6:17)

The host of heaven surrounded the enemy.

Elisha didn't say, "Look, God just created some angels." No, those angels were there all the time. You see, they existed in the invisible world all the time. Just because they were brought over in the physical, visible world, there is no reason to believe that angels had just been created! NO! We know that they already existed out there in the invisible world. God just manifested their presence by making them visible in the physical dimension.

Sometimes when we begin to experience healing, we say, "Oh, thank God, I got healed. I was healed at 10:30 in the morning yesterday."

No, you see, healing has existed for you ever since Jesus died and purchased it with His Blood. It has been yours for years. Salvation has been yours for years. Eternal life is yours. Healing is yours. Prosperity exists continually in another dimension. God will, through your faith, manifest it in the material realm.

Sometimes you do not see your healing. Sometimes you do not see your prosperity. Sometimes you do not feel your victory, but that does not mean it is not yours. Just as your angel is by your side and you are convinced by the Word of God that he lives in that invisible world watching after you, so too your healing is there. Your prosperity is there. As far as God is concerned, it is all yours. You can rejoice by your sense of faith that it is yours even though it has not yet been manifested.

Suppose I told my wife, Dodie, "Darling, I put $1,000.00 cash in your coat pocket for you to spend on whatever you want. It is in the coat hanging in the hall closet."

Do you know what Dodie would do? First of all, her heart would begin to rejoice because she believes me. Secondly, she would begin to make plans as to what to buy. Thirdly, she would begin talking about the fact of this blessing of $1,000. She would say, "I have a thousand dollars. I'm going to buy this and that. I'm just so excited about this wonderful blessing!"

Even though she does all those three things, she has not yet seen the thousand dollars. She has not yet smelled the thousand dollars. She has not yet tasted the thousand dollars. She has not yet felt the thousand dollars. She has not yet heard the rustle of the thousand dollars. Her natural senses have not had any contact with the thousand dollars at all. She only has the word of a person she trusts and loves.

What does she do? She believes. She talks, rejoices and makes plans, and yet she has no evidence except faith in my word.

Isn't it strange how people will act on the word of a husband, a lawyer, a doctor, or a wife and yet won't act on the Word of God? Man could lie, but God cannot lie!

As you walk out into the Word of God—the great forest of God's eternal truths—you will find out that God has put a lot in your pocket. He gave you salvation and healing for your body. He gave you prosperity and strength for physical tasks. He gave you victory and the ability to overcome satan. It is all out there in the spirit world. It is in your spiritual pocket. You have not yet touched it. You have not yet seen it. You have not yet felt it. All you have is the Word of Almighty God who cannot lie!

When you come back into the sense realm here in the visible world and begin to confess, "I am saved, all my debts are paid. I have strength, I am healed, I am delivered, I am blessed," you may not have any *physical* evidence for it. That should not bother you at all. You have been meditating in the Word of God and your spirit-man has seen it and reached out with the hand of faith to possess it. You can confidently say, "I have handled it by faith and I know it's mine."

You see, faith reaches out into the invisible area. It creates the physical realm out of invisible truths. All that we see was not made out of the visible but the invisible. All people of faith will be quick to tell you that prosperity, health, healing and salvation were not made out of visible things but of the invisible.

I want to show you this principle of faith reaching into the invisible world. Look again in Hebrews 11:1: "Now faith is the assurance, the confirmation, the title-deed of things we hope for, being the proof of things we do not see. Faith perceiving as real fact what is not revealed to the senses."

This is the first principle: Faith goes into the Word of God, believes God, and foresees as real fact what is not yet revealed to the five physical senses.

Hebrews 11:3, "By faith we understand that the worlds were framed, fashioned, put in order, and equipped for their intended purpose by the Word of God." The worlds were equipped and fashioned by the Word of God.

It would be silly for somebody to say, "Well, I don't believe in Bible reading. I don't believe in all of that." Some never go out in the forest of God's eternal truths and then wonder why they don't have any faith. They wonder why they don't have any ability to believe God. Oh, how this truth ought to make us live in the Word of God!

The Bible says that we understand that the things that are seen were made by the Word of God. The key is the Word of God.

You must start with the Word of God.

What we now see was not made out of things which are visible. The things that we see were made out of things which were invisible and became visible by the power of the Word of God.

Hebrews 11:6: "But without faith it is impossible to please God. For he that cometh to God must believe that He is." Do you mean to tell me that I am to believe that there is an invisible God?

The first principle of faith is believing that God is. God *is* an invisible person. Do you mean to tell me God expects me to believe what I can't see? He even asks you to believe that He exists when you can't see Him.

Why worry about financial prosperity that you do not yet see or a healing that you do not yet see? Why worry about that trouble that you do not see all worked out?

He that cometh to God must believe that the invisible IS.

THE INVISIBLE IS!

The first principle in getting anything out of the invisible world is to believe that it is, that it truly exists for you. Not only is God out there but every blessing we need is out there and the first principle to get anything is to believe that it IS. Is healing out there? Did Jesus die for your healing? Yes. Did Jesus die for your prosperity? Yes. Salvation? Yes. Blessings? Yes. Overcoming satan? Yes.

When you come to God you must believe that this invisible God is, that He truly exists. You must believe that this invisible God is a rewarder of those who diligently seek Him. (Hebrews 11:6) God is a rewarder.

God, the invisible person, is a rewarder of those who diligently seek Him. If He Himself, the invisible God, is a rewarder of those who diligently seek Him, isn't healing a reward if I diligently seek it? Isn't prosperity for me, if I diligently seek that invisible blessing? Are not all the overcoming factors mine if I diligently seek them?

Many times we will seek God diligently, but we will not seek the invisible blessings diligently. You might say, "I've been prayed for and I read the scriptures that they told me to confess for two days. I confessed for two days but all the time I was thinking, 'It's not

23

going to work. It's not going to work because I'm not getting any better'." You see, that's not diligently seeking God. The Bible says that we should read the Word of God and seek Him as for hidden treasure, as for gold and silver. (Proverbs 2:4)

If you will diligently seek any blessing you find in the Word of God, it will reward you by manifesting.

The faith man or woman, when it manifests, does not get all excited and say, "Glory to God, I got blessed today!" Instead, they say, "You know what happened, something showed up that I knew was already mine all the time." When your healing manifests and that knot disappears off your body, this is what you will say: "I'm glad it's physically gone, but with the eye of faith I have seen it gone ever since I read in the Bible, 'By His stripes ye were healed'. Healing has been mine ever since I found out about it." (Actually, it's been mine ever since Jesus died and rose again.)

When that day comes that you pay off your house, you will say: "It's been paid off for one year and six months, ever since I found out that God had supplied all my needs according to His riches in glory. I've been praising God continually because I saw it was paid off in that invisible world and now it's visible!"

He that cometh to God must believe that He is. We must believe the invisible God exists. Does God want me to believe in something I can't see? You can't see your healing or your financial blessing with your five natural senses. You must see by meditation in God's Word that He has given you these things. You have a right to them. First, you believe that they are in that invisible form, then in time they will be manifested materially.

Hebrews 11:7: "Prompted by faith Noah, being forewarned of God concerning events of which as yet there was *no visible sign,* took heed and diligently and reverently constructed and prepared an ark..." Noah was informed by God of events of which there was *no visible sign... as yet.* God informed Noah of events of which there was no *visible sign yet.*

You see, that's all that happens to us. I go out into the forest of God's great eternal truths and God says, "John Osteen, did you know that you are saved? Did you know that you are healed? Did you know you are blessed financially? Did you know that you are more than a conqueror? Did you know that you can lay hands on the sick and they will recover? Did you know in Jesus' Name you can cast out demons?"

God informs me of things and events of which there is yet no visible sign. Just because there is no visible sign yet does not mean you should not get happy. After God shows you these truths, you should say, "Oh I've been to God's information center. Hallelujah! I have information of which there is no visible sign. I found out from God that I am saved and going to heaven. I am washed from all of my sins. I am healed by His stripes. I am prosperous. I am more than a conqueror. I have inside information. I found it inside the Bible.It does not matter that there is not any visible sign, it's on its way! It's on its way!"

Hebrews 11:27, "Motivated by faith, he (Moses) left Egypt behind him, being unawed and undismayed by the wrath of the king; for he never flinched but held staunchly to his purpose and endured stedfastly as one who *gazed on Him Who is invisible.*"

Moses kept looking at the invisible God.

You keep gazing upon what is yours, whatever it is. If it is prosperity you want, keep gazing upon it in the invisible world as a blessing from God. Keep gazing upon health, if that is where you have a need. Keep stedfastly looking upon victory if that is what you want. Keep stedfastly looking upon yourself as being well and healed and your entire family living for God. Keep gazing stedfastly at the invisible blessing and you will endure all opposition and it will become yours.

Hebrews 11:32: "And what shall I say further? For time would fail me to tell of Gideon, Barak, Samson, Jephthah, of David and Samuel and the prophets."

Let's look at Gideon's life. Gideon was sitting behind the wine press threshing wheat for fear of the enemies of Israel. He was frustrated, fearful, discouraged, and feeling like a failure. God sent an angel down to him. This angel didn't say, "Hail thou scaredy-cat. Hail thou cringing coward!"

He came to him with news from the other world and said, "Hail thou mighty man of valour!"

Gideon said, "Who else is here? Do you mean to tell me that I am a mighty man of valour?"

Now the angel could have said, and might well have said, "Yes, that is exactly how God sees you. It's all yours whether you ever take it or not. You are a mighty man of valour. I bring you news from the spirit world!"

Gideon rose up and began to act like he was a mighty man of valour and he found out he was!

Well, God came to me and said, "Hail, John Osteen, thou mighty man, healed by the stripes of

26

Jesus." I could have answered, "Are you sure you are talking to me? I sure don't feel like it."

Yes, in the spirit world, God Almighty sees you healed. He sees you prosperous. He sees you strong. He sees you victorious. Rise up and begin to act like it's yours and it will leap into being!

This is the exact principle that Jesus Christ was teaching in Mark 11:24. "Therefore I say unto you, What things soever ye desire, when ye pray ... (When you pray ... that is when you are sick, that is when you are defeated, that is when you have darkness over you.) ... believe that ye receive them, (in the invisible form) and ye shall have them (in the visible form)."

Jesus does not ask you to go around lying and saying, "I believe that knot is gone physically from my body." No, He does not ask you to tell a lie. Anybody with eyes could see that the knot is still there. He does not ask you to believe that it is already manifested in the physical realm. He asks you to believe it is yours in the invisible realm on the basis of God's Word. Then, He said that He will see that you get it in the visible, physical form.

BELIEVE YOU RECEIVE IN THE FAITH REALM AND YOU SHALL HAVE IT IN THE NATURAL REALM.

Many times when you say that you believe you have received your healing, it does not mean you can say that you believe that you do not hurt, or that you believe that there are no symptoms in your body. But your faith, the sense of smell for the perfume, reaches out into the invisible world and you simply say, "I believe, after walking in the forest of God's eternal

27

truths and I am convinced that God's will is my healing. I have been healed by the stripes of Jesus Christ and healing is mine in the invisible world. It's mine now!''

My business is to believe it is mine and to confess it, rejoice about it and act like it. Jesus' business is to see that it is manifested! These are the building blocks of faith.

Ephesians 1:3 tells us, ''Blessed be the God and Father of our Lord Jesus Christ, who hath blessed us with ALL spiritual blessings...'' How many? ALL! For many years I did not enjoy ALL God's blessings. I would say, ''Lord, why don't you give me some financial and physical blessings? I don't understand why blessings have to be so spiritual.''

Now I have discovered and understand the wisdom of God, in that God has blessed me with all the creative building blocks of the universe. He has blessed us with all spiritual blessings in the heavenly places. They are all ours! We simply walk with God, find out what is ours and take it.

In II Corinthians 4:18, Paul the Apostle is talking about how he lived. This is a marvelous verse of scripture to meditate on, ''Since we consider and look not to the things that are seen but to the things that are unseen; for the things that are visible are temporal, brief, fleeting (subject to change), but the things that are invisible are deathless and everlasting.''

We are to join hands with the Creator of the universe.

All that you see was not made out of visible things, but out of invisible things. You must begin in the invisible realm of God's truth and let it affect your

28

spirit man. It will bring into reality that which you desire.

God is a Creator. He wants His sons and daughters to join hands with Him to see His miraculous power create things for their every need. He wants to help them reach the world with the good news about Jesus. The building blocks for God's creative power are not in the natural realm. His building blocks are in another dimension. All that you need from God you can obtain through the use of your sixth sense of faith. You can bring the blessing of God out of the invisible, spirit world, into the material realm where you live TODAY!

BOOKS BY JOHN OSTEEN

A Miracle For Your Marriage
A Place Called There
ABC's of Faith
Believing God For Your Loved Ones
Deception! Recognizing True and False Ministries
Four Principles in Receiving From God
*Healed of Cancer by Dodie Osteen
*How To Claim the Benefits of the Will
How To Demonstrate Satan's Defeat
How To Flow in the Super Supernatural
How To Minister Healing to the Sick
*How To Receive Life Eternal
How To Release the Power of God
Keep What God Gives
Love & Marriage
Overcoming Hindrances To Receiving the Baptism in the Holy Spirit
Overcoming Opposition: How To Succeed in Doing the Will of God
    by Lisa Comes
*Pulling Down Strongholds
*Receive the Holy Spirit
Reigning in Life as a King
Rivers of Living Water
Saturday's Coming
Seven Facts About Prevailing Prayer
Seven Qualities of a Man of Faith
*Six Lies the Devil Uses To Destroy Marriages by Lisa Comes
Spiritual Food For Victorious Living
The Believer's #1 Need
The Bible Way to Spiritual Power
The Confessions of a Baptist Preacher
*The Divine Flow
*The 6th Sense...Faith
The Truth Shall Set You Free
*There Is a Miracle in Your Mouth
This Awakening Generation
Unraveling the Mystery of the Blood Covenant
*What To Do When Nothing Seems To Work
What To Do When the Tempter Comes
You Can Change Your Destiny

*Also available in Spanish.

Please write for a complete list of prices in the John Osteen Library.
Lakewood Church • P.O. Box 23297 • Houston, Texas 77228